Going Vegan - How To Vegan Without Going Crazy

Dr. Robertino Bedenian

Published by Dr. Robertino Bedenian, 2024.

GOING VEGAN - HOW TO VEGAN WITHOUT GOING CRAZY

First edition. January 13, 2024.

Copyright © 2024 Dr. Robertino Bedenian.

ISBN: 979-8224597130

Written by Dr. Robertino Bedenian.

Also by Dr. Robertino Bedenian

Fitness Over 60 For Women – How to Stay Fit And Healthy As You Age

Does Back Pain Go Away? 10 Answers To The Most Acute Back Pain Issues

Massage Bible - A Beginners Guide To Western And Eastern Massage Therapy

Going Vegan - How To Vegan Without Going Crazy

Chiropraktik - Was Steckt Eigentlich Dahinter?

Massagen: Ein Überblick Über Westliche Und Östliche Massagetechniken

Natuerlich Abnehmen, Schlank Und Endlich Fit Sein

P.S. Ich Liebe Dich: Wenn Liebe So Einfach Wäre

Was Tun Bei Rückenschmerzen, Bandscheibenvorfall Und Ischiasschmerzen: 10 Antworten Zu Den Häufigsten Fragen Bei Rückenschmerzen

Was Tun Gegen Schlafapnoe, Schlafstörungen Und Schnarchen

Self-Help Books for Women

Diabetes How to Help: Everything You Need to Know About Diabetes Type 1 and Type 2

Diet and Workout Planner: How to Stay Healthy and Get Fit for Life

Everything I Know About Love

The Sleep Easy Solution Book: How to Stop Sleep Apnea, Snoring, and Sleep Disorders

Your Super Gut Feeling Restored – How to Restore Your Life Energy and Overall Health from The Inside Out

Table of Contents

GOING VEGAN

How To Vegan Without Going Crazy

Dr. Robertino Bedenian

Copyright

1

INTRODUCTION: SO, WHAT IS VEGAN COOKING ALL ABOUT?

People in our modern-day culture are interested in a several issues. Wellness and the environment are two popular ones that seem to be have top priority. Individuals wish to eat well and reduce their environmental impact. Hazards of global warming and weight problems are two of the most severe troubles.

Some individuals choose they want to take on both at the same time. Making the option to end up being a vegan is a choice that is made equally for wellness and environmental reasons. Vegan food preparation is just food prepared within the vegan specifications to support that way of living.

HOW DO I GET STARTED?

Attempting to create a new eating practice and change to veganism is something that even more people are trying to do yearly. From a lifestyle that used to be fairly uncommon, it has grown into a lot more well-liked alternative and is gaining a gigantic amount of support in all lines of business. Individuals who work on several jobs, individuals who reside in multi-million-dollar houses as well as the rebelling young adult down the block are all likely to be vegans nowadays. With a lot of people relying on veganism, no doubt that you have also questioned at some point in your life what it would mean for you if you should also take this route.

The majority of individuals believe that veganism is more or less like vegetarianism. This is simply inaccurate. They are two entirely different lifestyles that just share a few similarities. Generally speaking, vegetarianism is a much less complicated way of living to embrace and less rigid. Veganism is much more stringent and more challenging for somebody to adapt to. This can make it very complicated to alter to vegan living immediately.

So, to reap the full benefits of living as a vegan, it is crucial to adhere to all the tips. This indicates staying away from all foods and food products that consist of animals, or are made from animal components. This includes meat, honey, milk, eggs, cheese, natural yogurt, and various other comparable items. A real vegan diet plan will consist of gigantic amounts of bread, vegetables, fruits, pasta, and similar meals. This can be an incredibly revolutionary diet plan for a person to follow who is used to consume big portions of meat. So, it could be a bit hard in the beginning.

That is why you should start making these diet adjustments gradually to make the entire procedure as simple as possible. The suggestion of a single huge change may seem simpler, yet in reality, this is normally a whole lot more challenging and is related to a considerably higher risk of failing to follow up with the vegan way of living. Rather the smaller modifications are even better given that they will certainly lay the structure for permanent changes.

Not every person thinks that switching to vegan cooking is to be considered a calamity. Some individuals switch over to the brand-new diet plan with no troubles or complications whatsoever. Nevertheless, individuals who usually enjoy a more convenient diet "transition" are those who use to eat small amounts of meat and various other animal products regularly. This makes it easier for them to adapt to this brand-new lifestyle with the least amount of complication. If you find that you are having an issue adjusting to the new dietary demands, you should constantly take some time to see if there are any kind of small changes you could make to your life to make things easier.

These small changes could appear small to you, yet they can considerably help you achieve your goal. Waiting until you have completely failed the diet plan, can be extremely frustrating. Looking for as much help as possible and as fast as possible is rather a great attitude to have and is normally quite easy to do. A few moments of your time is everything you are asked for. The outcomes are well worth the initiative, and you will certainly be glad you took that time. Your brand-new vegan way of living awaits you, as long as you can take care of the transition.

WHAT DOES IT MEAN TO BE VEGAN?

Veganism is a part of vegetarianism. There are different types of vegetarianism. Some vegetarians still consume milk and/or eat eggs. However, vegans do not do so. They are the strictest type and do not consider ANY animal products in their diet.

It is the most daunting kind of diet since people are often relatively strictly adapted to their diet habits. Eggs and milk, for instance, prevail over baking ingredients. So, replacements are required to be made if a vegan is supposed to consume them.

HOW WILL I KNOW IF MY FOOD IS VEGAN OR NOT?

For meals to be purely vegan, they have to adhere to specific requirements. It is essential to keep in mind that there are a lot of unknown components in meals. It is specifically vital to look out for those components if you take the vegan diet seriously.

a) Vegans do not consume animal products or by-products of animal products.

b) They also do not drink milk or eat eggs.

c) Real vegans even avoid fish.

d) Do not overlook that bees are also animals, so vegans do not eat honey, imperial jelly, and bee pollen supplements, too.

e) There are likewise plenty of hidden ingredients to keep an eye out for that usually make their way into meals, including gelatin, lard, and whey.

If you are a new vegan, making all these modifications might seem frustrating. However, after you have been consuming and cooking the vegan way for some time you will become a professional very quickly.

WHAT YOU SHOULD KNOW AFTER READING THIS BOOK

There is no question that a vegetarian diet regimen, particularly a vegan one, could be terrific for your health. However, with the rising establishments of natural food stores as a result of an awareness that a lot of people are planning to improve their wellness, it is simpler than ever to delight in a rewarding vegan diet plan. This book is created to show you ways how to accomplish that, such as:

1) The fundamentals of ways to cook vegan meals properly.

2) An outline of regular components used in vegan food preparation.

3) A list of hidden ingredients you should stay away from while following a vegan diet regimen.

4) Information on ways how to equip your kitchen "vegan-like" to prepare vegan recipes every day without a problem.

5) Cooking techniques are required to produce a range of delightful dishes.

6) Ways to rustle a complete vegan meal while getting the appropriate harmony of supplements, minerals, and nutrients for your optimal health.

7) Recommendations on what exactly to do if you have special nutritional requirements, such as those who have diabetic issues or higher cholesterol levels.

8) Recipes you could start cooking immediately.

As you can see, there is a great deal of information to take advantage of for the best ways to take pleasure in a vegan diet regimen. This book is made to instruct you on every little thing you need to understand when it comes to living a vegan life successfully.

2

VEGAN COOKING IS HEALTHY COOKING

As you know by now, vegan food preparation is cooking that is done without meat, fish, eggs, or by-products of any one of these items. To support a vegan way of living, special cautiousness is required to ensure that none of these ingredients make their way into the food.

We take specific things for granted. For instance: Have you ever given a second thought about avoiding eggs while baking? Probably not. However, this is about to change. Well, eggs are not allowed throughout a vegan diet plan. Although the vegan way of living becomes more popular, you might face some challenges when it comes to getting these packaged vegan meals. To resolve this trouble, many vegans choose to do their very own food preparation.

This book is going to focus on numerous different sorts of ingredients starting with ways to change milk and eggs with vegan products. After this, it is going to also cover information about other components that are used as well as animal by-products to look out for.

ALL BEGINNINGS ARE DIFFICULT: RECIPES WITHOUT EGGS

As much as we would like to stay away from using eggs in our vegan dishes, it can turn out to be a very strenuous task. Eggs are among the most difficult ingredients to replace. Nonetheless, there are numerous alternatives to choose from that will certainly take care of the job.

THE BINDING POWER OF EGGS

In specific dishes, eggs are virtually vital. They bind ingredients with each other. They can be used to make baked products and contribute to making them light and fluffy. Additionally, eggs are valued for their ability to give some structure to the product and to provide sufficient moisture. They are specifically useful while baking and are also necessary for certain delicious meals.

YOU STILL HAVE A CHOICE

Right here is a checklist of several of the most effective egg replacement choices around. You can replace the eggs in any recipe by making use of these alternatives.

Use Pureed Bananas

Pureed bananas are yet another efficient egg substitute. Just put a split banana in the mixer and pulse up until entirely smooth and there are no lumps. A half banana is a substitute for one egg.

The favorable aspect of using bananas is that they are easily available. However, bananas have a peculiar flavor that might not fit with every dish. As an example, if you were trying to make peanut butter cookies, the banana taste would change the flavor.

Ground Flaxseeds

It is highly recommended to acquire the flax seeds whole and keep them in the fridge. When it is time to use them, take one tablespoon of flaxseeds for each egg that you require to replace. Then, put it in a mixer or coffee grinder.

Move the flax seeds to a bowl and add three tablespoons of water for every egg you require to replace. Add the water gradually while whisking vigorously. Whisk up until the combination takes a gel-like shape.

Because flax seeds are nutty-tasting, this egg replacement serves best when making things like whole-grain bread, buns, and pancakes. You may want to experiment with the different sorts of dishes you like this to be in.

Egg Substitute Product

There are several egg replacement products out on the market that are created to be vegan-like. Take inventory of the product packaging to be sure that it is vegan risk-free, and that it also does not include any type of meat.

These egg replacement powders are used with mingled feelings. Some are fond of them; others just cannot get used to them. They are beneficial and great to have on hand. Once you start cooking vegan regularly, you will begin to find out which meals should involve them and which do not.

Given that there are several brands on the market, it may take a while to look at one that you are satisfied with. When using, merely follow the package instructions. They normally are available in powder form. If you cannot get it at the health-food store, you could conveniently get it online.

Try Tofu As An Egg Substitute

Tofu is likewise another alternative you could try if you are looking out for a replacement product. In the beginning, you could experiment with any kind of tofu. However, this could take some time. Silken tofu appears to generate the very best outcome. You could also use unflavored soya natural yogurt in the same proportion with similar outcomes.

The great thing about tofu is that it blends well with many tastes. Flax seeds, for example, have that unique nutty taste. Tofu does not have a great deal of flavor by itself, particularly when combined with stronger ingredients. One more benefit is that it is extensively available in many areas, also in ordinary supermarkets.

To make use of it, simply take the tofu and mix it in the mixer. Make sure that there are no lumps and the structure is as smooth as possible. To replace one huge egg, make use of 1/4 cup of the mixture.

It will take some trials and errors to see which recipes operate best with tofu as an egg substitute. Everything depends on the kinds of dishes you try and on your taste.

Utilizing Flour And Other Leavening Means

You could also take advantage of pastes made from different types of flours, and leavening means to substitute the eggs. The advantage is that these components are available in many kitchens. Additionally, they do not have the flavor of bananas and flaxseeds. That is why they can be mixed into the concoction rather well.

Again, it could take some time of trying until you get the proportions right. Below are some options:

1 tablespoon flour of any kind (wheat flour, oat flour, or soy flour) and 1 tablespoon water for every egg.

1 tablespoon baking powder, 1 tablespoon flour, 2 tablespoons water for every egg.

2 tablespoons corn starch and 2 tablespoons water mixed also replace one egg.

Finding The Right Egg Substitute

Once more, as you try these various mixes, you will get an idea of which egg replacement works best for which recipe. In the beginning, you should start with one of your preferred meals and try out various egg alternatives until the flavor and texture you desire are reached.

For instance, if you wish to make a group of blueberry muffins, you could replace the eggs with any type of these substitution choices. Find out how it tastes. Next time you make it, try an additional egg substitute. After several attempts, you should decide which had been your preferred one and stick to that. Pretty quickly, you will have the ability to discern at a glance which egg replacement product works best for certain sorts of dishes.

HOW TO REPLACE MILK

For a vegan, milk from any type of animal (sheep, cow, goat, etc.) is additionally restricted. It is likewise a quite common ingredient with baking and food preparation. Milk is also much less complicated to replace than eggs.

To replace milk in recipes, just substitute any one of these vegan options. For example, if the dish asks for one cup of milk, use rather one cup of soy milk. Below are some different milk alternatives:

Soy Milk

Soy milk is available in a wide range of flavors and is readily offered. Flavors include vanilla, unsweetened, delicious chocolate, and even egg nog. Some brands are thicker and creamier compared to others. You might have to do some trying out before you find the brands that suit best to you. Unless it has a unique flavor, soy milk is fairly neutral and blends well in recipes. Soy milk is likewise abundant in healthy protein.

Nut Milk

Nut milk drinks such as almond milk and hazelnut milk are additional options. Unlike soy milk, nut milk has a distinct flavor and might not fit well with every dish. There is sweetened and bitternut milk, too.

Rice Milk

Rice milk additionally provides a fantastic option to substitute milk in recipes. Rice milk has a very light taste and blends well in recipes. Nevertheless, it is essential to note that rice milk normally does not include a lot of healthy protein, so you should make sure to compensate for that from another source.

The more you get used to these various tastes of milk substitute products, the more you will intuitively know what fits best with your dish.

HOW TO REPLACE BUTTERMILK

Buttermilk is also a vital ingredient used in many various recipes. For a vegan, using buttermilk is not allowed as it is an animal product. Buttermilk is merely normal milk that has been cultured, which means that it has some good microorganisms in it similar to yogurt.

Fortunately, you can easily make your own. The process is as follows. It makes one cup of vegan-friendly buttermilk.

1) Put one cup of soy milk in a Pyrex glass.

2) Include 1 tablespoon of white vinegar or lemon juice and mix.

3) Allow it to sit for about fifteen minutes before using it.

Soy milk works the very best. Rice milk and nut milk do not work so well. The chemistry of soy milk is much better suited.

HOW TO REPLACE BUTTER AND LARD

Butter is yet another essential ingredient that is included in a lot of recipes. There are many various things you can do to substitute it:

Vegetable Oil

If the dish calls for melted and even solid butter, you should consider using vegetable oil instead. This, nevertheless, may change the structure of the recipe a little so you will need to experiment in the beginning.

Shortening

If you need a strong fat to use in recipes, you could take advantage of vegan-friendly shortening. However, this is a manufactured product and filled with trans fats. So, using it in moderation is best. Shortening is not great for you whatsoever! You could also take butter-flavored shortening if the meal is supposed to be butter-tasting.

Margarine

This is another alternative that could replace butter or various other strong fats, specifically if you prefer something with a buttery flavor. However, margarine is also higher in trans fats. Watch for trans fat-free products, but even those might consist of remains of trans fats.

Reducing Fat

Additionally, you can lessen fat with fruit purees. For instance, if the dish requires one cup of butter, you could use 1/2 cup apple dressing and 1/2 cup vegan margarine or shortening. Other fruit purees you can make use of include plum puree and banana puree. You could also be lucky and discover different fat replacing fruit purees in the shop. Just make sure that they are vegan-friendly and follow the directions to replace them properly. You may also wish to attempt to replace the fat in the recipe with fruit. However, this could alter the texture way too much.

Constantly, make sure that butter substituting products are used in small amounts. A diet that is high in fat and trans fats is not healthy and balanced. If you require them, use them only occasionally.

THE TYPICAL INGREDIENTS OF VEGAN COOKING

Vegan food preparation is an art. As shown in the previous chapter, components such as milk, buttermilk, eggs, and butter are virtually important for recipes. But, as we discovered, the substitutions are more than adequate. With that stated, there are many ingredients that a lot of vegan cooks think to be crucial. Right here is a rundown of several of the most usual ones.

Soy Products

Soy is possibly the most versatile plant available, specifically because it helps to provide healthy and high in protein vegan dishes. Listed here is a list of some of the available soy products:

Soy Milk

Soy milk can be purchased almost everywhere and can be selected in many different tastes, such as vanilla and delicious chocolate.

Tofu

Tofu is available at different levels of firmness such as an extra firm or soft.

Tempeh

Tempeh is a fermented product with a hearty, meaty texture that can be made use of in French fries and various other dishes.

Ground Meat Substitute

This soy product is a staple to some since you can make dishes such as Spaghetti Bolognese and vegan chili.

Soy Yogurt

This is available with active cultures just like regular yogurt and comes in with a variety of flavors.

Miso

Miso is a fermented salty paste that is made from soy and is used as a popular, rich in the enzyme soup base.

Tamari And Soy Sauce

Both products are made from soy.

Edamame

These are soybeans and excellent by themselves or in French fries.

Soy Cheese

Soy cheese even melts and has a comparable structure as real cheese.

Soy Sausage, Hot Dogs, And Hamburger Patties

Vegans do not need to abstain from breakfast sausage, hot dogs, as well as hamburger patties.

Soy Chick

They can be found in a wide range of types, such as patties, nuggets, and so on.

Soy Protein Powder

Soy protein provides an excellent method to raise your day-to-day healthy protein intake. You can put a scoop in your early-morning smoothie mix, or include it in dishes such as pancakes and bread.

Soy Flour

This is also an important product, particularly for baking.

There is a wide range of soy products out there, and this list should not be considered as a complete checklist. It just illustrates the flexibility of the food products. Seek soy products that are used from non-genetically modified soybeans.

However, soy products do also have their critics. Some only like to use them "traditionally", for instance as tofu, tempeh, miso, edamame, and tamari. Opponents of processed soy products do not seem to like the idea that they are created to taste like meat or milk products, which to them opposes the aim of being vegan. Plus, these meals tend to be strongly processed, which does not necessarily make them healthier. Whether or not you consider taking advantage of them, is a decision that you need to make after balancing the advantages and disadvantages.

Whole Grains

There are numerous and various kinds of whole grains out there. So, it is worthwhile to experiment. Grains are rich in vitamins, minerals, fiber, and other crucial nutrients. They also have healthy protein, specifically quinoa - an old grain that is particularly rich in protein. Listed here are some whole-grain products you could try out:

Rye

Buckwheat

Quinoa

Wheat Products

Pasta

Brown Rice

Oats

These can be ground into flour or used whole. They should be the backbone of a healthy and balanced vegan diet.

Nuts And Seeds

These are also very crucial components of a healthy vegan diet. They are rich in minerals and vitamins and healthy and balanced fats. Here is a listing of some nuts and seeds:

Hazelnuts

Walnuts

Sunflower Seeds

Pumpkin Seeds

Pecans

Almonds

Cashews

Sesame Seeds

Poppy Seeds

Flax Seeds

Hemp Seeds

You can include them in dishes and also consume them on their own as a snack.

Legumes

Legumes are a necessary protein source for a vegan, specifically when paired with whole grains. They should be combined to provide a full protein. If they should be among your main protein sources, it is very important to bear in mind to incorporate them.

Right here are some instances. This list is by no means complete:

Chick Peas (garbanzo beans)

Lentils

Kidney beans

Black Beans

Cannelloni Beans

Northern Beans

Black-Eyes Peas

Split Peas

You could discover legumes in dried-out kind, ground-in to flour, and canned. The dried kind requires to be soaked overnight to soften it. The canned kind is easy to use and fantastic to have on hand. Flour is also a popular ingredient in baked foods and is tasty for food preparation.

Fruits And Vegetables

Very important to your health are fruits and vegetables. They add color and variety to your meals. As a vegan, your entire diet will certainly be plant-based, so you need to get your share of vitamins, minerals, and nutrients from things like vegetables and fruits.

Try to find organic products whenever feasible as they will make your meals even healthier. Organic food is also much better for the environment.

Canned And Packaged Foods

As the vegan diet is on the rise, so is the availability of packaged, vegan-friendly meals. For example, here is a list of some of the things you can look out for:

Bread

Desserts

Baked Goods

Snacks

Vegan Chocolate

Canned Goods

Beverages

Breakfast Foods And Cereals

Etc.

The great thing to know is that you do not even have to go to an organic food store to find a lot of these products. Indeed, organic food stores have a lot of vegan alternatives, but you can even locate vegan products in your regular grocery store.

Right here is a fantastic source that will certainly offer you a list of all the vegan foods you could discover at the supermarket:

http://www.peta.org/accidentallyVegan/

Print it out to make sure that you can discover the things that you require when you go to the shop. We will examine a few of these products in more detail as we discuss the best ways to equip a full vegan pantry.

THE INGREDIENTS THEY USE TO HIDE FROM YOU

As discussed in a previous section, there are usually hidden ingredients in foods that are animal results. A real vegan will take the additional step required to investigate exactly what these components are and avoid them.

If it is a packaged meal and it is listed as being vegan-friendly, you can be fairly positive that the meal does not have these components in it. However, do not let this marking prevent you from checking though.

Here is a checklist of the ingredients to look out for. There are two types of components - those that are obviously from animal products, and those that could be from animal products.

If you have any doubts, the only way to check is by contacting the supplier of the food product. And if they do not know, you should consider not buying their products as they might not be risk-free.

Ingredients From Animals

These ingredients are rather common in products. So, if a product is not classified as vegan, you ought to examine the ingredients list to make sure they are not included.

Albumin - comes from egg whites

Milk Products - includes whey protein powder, lactase, lactose, and things like milk and dried milk

Calcium Caseinate – a fairly common additive

Calcium Stearate – also another additive

Suet – a type of animal fat

Tallow – animal fat product is made from suet

Bee products – this includes royal jelly, propolis, honey, and bee pollen

Carmine – a food additive that comes from insects

Lard – a type of animal fat

Casein – this is the protein that is in cheese

Gelatin – from animals, a popular product found especially in jellies and desserts

<u>Other common hidden ingredients from animals include:</u>

Cochineal

Isinglass

Muriatic acid

Oleic acid

Palmitic acid

Pancreatin

Pepsin

Most of these ingredients listed above are typically blended as additives in food. They have different purposes depending on the food that they are added to.

Ingredients That May Be From Animals

The following ingredients serve different functions in the meals that they are in. Some are classified as additives. Others emulsify foods and provide additional fats. However, please note that some products sound like animal components, but this does not necessarily mean these components are animal products. They could be artificially manufactured or come from plants. You will need to check it out.

<u>These ingredients include:</u>

Emulsifying agents

Fatty acid

Adipic acid

Glyceride

Glycerol

Capric acid

Lactic acid

Magnesium stearate

Monoglyceride

Anything listed as "natural flavoring"

Clarifying agents

Disodium inosinate

Glyceride

Glycerol

Stearic acid

Diglyceride

Polysorbate

Sodium stearoyl lactylate

Indeed, a few of those ingredients are hard to pronounce - several of them do not even seem to be food! They all have various purposes in the foods that we consume daily. We just do not think about these individual purposes they have. The point is that if you wish to enjoy a vegan way of living, you will need to go the extra mile and check if your favored meals might contain the animal variations of these ingredients.

Moreover, it is essential to understand that the components pointed out in this section can be found in almost everything. If you try to concentrate too much on it, it may get very frustrating. It is very important to live a balanced life, meaning that the vegan lifestyle must not make you think that you are missing out on a fulfilling life. You will have to find your spot between living as a vegan and a vegan-free lifestyle. Only if you have found this spot and feel comfortable with where you are, you will have a very good chance to continue your vegan trip.

Being a vegan is a dedication to a different lifestyle. Finding out about the meals you should consume as a vegan, how you can make vegan-friendly substitutions with baking and cooking, and all about the hidden components you need to abstain from are all crucial steps towards living the vegan life successfully.

3

OKAY, HOW DO I GET INTO THIS VEGAN COOKING?

Establishing your pantry is a crucial step to prepare dishes spontaneously. For people who have been vegetarians all their lives, setting up the pantry might not be a struggle anymore. However, if you have made up your mind lately to live the vegan lifestyle, you will probably encounter some challenges you will have to master. You might have some ingredients available, yet most of your kitchen may not be set up for a vegan lifestyle.

This listing will certainly not include easily perishable products such as fruits and vegetables. Nevertheless, also some perishable items, such as certain brands of tofu, soy milk, rice milk, almond milk, etc. can be kept on the shelves and not in the fridge as a result of the special product packaging.

FIRST: CHECK WHAT YOU HAVE

The initial step to set up a vegan pantry is to take stock of what you have. This step is usually for those who have lately decided to be vegans. Nonetheless, if you have been vegan for a while, you will certainly also take advantage of this. The target is to think about everything that you have and to identify if it assists the vegan way of life.

You might also intend to review the ingredients' checklists of all your packaged meals to figure out if any of the hidden components discussed in the previous chapter are included. Even if you have been vegan for a while, you could still discover some foods in your pantry that should not be available in your kitchen store.

In case you happen to spot some food you need to get rid of but have not been opened yet, do not throw them away. Give them to a community that offers meals to the deserving poor. Just because you will certainly not eat them does not imply that someone else will not profit from them and cherish having something to consume.

SECOND: START WITH WHAT YOU NEED

It is not essential to have a big pantry piled up with lots of ingredients and packaged foods. All you have to do is sit and think about the things that are crucial to you. If you should not cook that often, never mind buying cooking supplies until you need them. If you are the sort of individual who happens to like cereal and has a few bowls a day, you may want to keep packages of nut milk, soy milk, rice milk, and cereal in your pantry so you do not need to rush to the store continuously.

After you have exactly determined what you need and what your food preferences are, you can begin buying the products to put in your kitchen. If you do not take the extra time to consider what you need, you will wind up buying things you will never eat. Then, the food will go to waste. Simply stock the basics and if you need anything, you could buy it later.

THIRD: STOCK UP YOUR PANTRY GRADUALLY

It could get very expensive to stock your pantry at one time. There are certain components that you may need now and then, such as tomato sauce and various other products. It is not essential to get many of these items in the beginning. You could add them to your kitchen bit by bit as you go shopping, or as you need them for your next vegan meal.

Of course, it is comfortable to always have the ingredients available to make a couple of easy meals such as pasta recipes, soups, and grain and vegetable dinners. Think about the sort of meals you would like to consume and then purchase the necessary ingredients.

You could buy these items when you start the week off and store them after you have bought them.

YOUR PERFECT VEGAN COOKING COULD LOOK LIKE THIS

Although pantries might differ in every household, it would be handy to see an example pantry. You could use this as a starting point while trying to find out ways to equip yours, or you can take this listing to the store and start buying! It depends on you.

It might help to think about your pantry regarding classifications such as morning meal items, snacks, and so on. Here is an example list:

Breakfast

Whole-grain warm cereals, such as oatmeal or cream of wheat

Cold cereals to eat with soy milk, nut milk, or rice milk

Vegan-friendly pancake blends

Vegan cooked products such as muffins

Snacks

A selection of healthy and balanced snack items such as granola bars

Vegan snacks such as biscuits and cakes

Cookies and various other baked products

Miscellaneous Products

Nut milk, soy milk, rice milk, and tofu are in special packaging to help them store in the pantry so they remain longer fresh

Canned soups, soup blends, and other boxed dish items such as vegan macaroni and cheese

Nuts and seeds such as almonds, sesame seeds, sunflower seeds, and pecans

Noodles - search for whole-wheat varieties

Products like pasta sauce, capers, pickles, ketchup, salad dressings, and so on

Grain Products

These are just a few examples listed below. Buy products that are following your choices:

Whole-wheat rice

Buckwheat flour

Wheat flour

Quinoa

Condiments

One vegetable oil to cook with

At least one type of flavorful oil such as cold-pressed olive oil or roasted sesame oil

Tamara and/or soy sauce

Vinegar - you can keep many kinds available, such as balsamic, rice wine, and red wine vinegar

Salt, pepper, and natural herbs and spices

Baking Products

Leavening agents such as yeast, baking powder, and baking soda

Vegan-friendly egg replacement

Different types of flours

Sugars and other sweetener products such as maple syrup and rice syrup

This checklist is merely designed to offer you a starting point. It is virtually impossible to cover all items in a list because peoples' food inclinations differ significantly. The approach most individuals like to take is purchasing products one by one as they need them.

Do not forget to consider the components, especially when you are purchasing packaged meals. As we have discovered, there are frequently hidden ingredients where you would expect them least that are not vegan-friendly.

4

STARTING YOUR VEGAN COOKING ADVENTURE

So, we took some time thinking about some of the common components that are usually included in vegan meals. We have suggested ways to stock the kitchen as well as to find unknown ingredients in meals that vegans are not supposed to eat.

The upcoming step is to discover ways to prepare these meals.

If you already know how to cook, you could skip this chapter. However, I would advise reading it anyway since there could be things in right here you could still profit from. To get this right just from the very beginning, it is recommended to start preparing these meals with people who know what they are doing, so you can learn from them.

Alternatively, you can take some food preparation classes. Search around on the internet to see if you can find any sort of vegan cooking courses that could give you a great introduction to a few of these techniques.

Even though we are going to discuss the strategies you should know when it comes to preparing vegan foods in this chapter, it could be much more fun to learn about that in a group atmosphere.

Here is a standard listing of several of the strategies you need to follow:

a) How to set up your kitchen properly

b) How to read recipes

c) Basic cooking techniques

Individuals could spend a lifetime finding out ways how to prepare meals and not even scratch the surface. So, we will go over several of the fundamental procedures. If you want to discover more about that, you should probably consider enrolling in a course.

IS YOUR KITCHEN WELL-EQUIPPED FOR VEGAN COOKING?

As pointed out in the previous chapter, stocking your pantry is a crucial part of the vegan cooking puzzle. The other is to have a well-equipped kitchen to prepare any kind of dishes on demand.

Now, there are two sorts of cooks out there. Those who use to take advantage of a variety of devices, and those who do not. As a rule, most of them tend to drop somewhere in-between.

Below is a checklist of several of the fundamental kitchen area materials you should have on hand to be able to prepare a variety of recipes.

1) A good mixture of knives that involve a bread knife and a chef's knife. Unless they are serrated, make sure you keep them sharp. You will need a huge cutting board.

2) An electric mixer. If you use to do a lot of baking, make sure to have an upright mixer that sits on your countertop.

3) A variety of utensils, such as a pair of strong thongs, a sieve, wooden spoons, rubber spatulas, and a strong wire whisk.

4) A small toaster oven and a microwave

5) A blender and/or a mixer

6) Optional, but wonderful to have on hand - a mixer, ice cream machine, a slicer if you cannot do without fresh-baked bread

7) A good mixture of pots, pans, baking recipes, and blending bowls

Some individuals make the mistake of getting every little thing at the same time. This is a mistake, particularly if you are brand-new to food preparation. You will begin to understand your individual preferences over time.

STICK TO THE RULES: READ THE RECIPES

Knowing how to follow dishes is a crucial prerequisite to finding out about the best ways how to prepare vegan meals. Many recipes are pretty uncomplicated. Nonetheless, it is easy to take them for granted until something goes wrong. There are many handwritten recipes out there that overlook critical components without purpose. If you discover a dish similar to this, having great knowledge of just how dishes work can help you tremendously to find out about the missing ingredient.

If you are simply learning how to prepare, you will find yourself sticking to recipes most of the time. However, as you become more familiar with cooking, you will slowly start to become independent of them.

After you have followed some recipes several times, you could even start to write your very own original dishes down. However, make sure to include the ingredients in the order that they will show up in the preparation guidelines. This makes the dish less complicated to prepare.

COOKING TECHNIQUES YOU SHOULD KNOW BEFORE STARTING COOKING

After you established your kitchen and became confident about how to follow recipes properly, you will also need to find out about some fundamental food preparation techniques. Below is a list of a few of those things you will need to do to cook.

The Best Ways How To Use Your Knives

There is a right and wrong way to cut. A lot of people do not seem to wonder about that. Nonetheless, applying the wrong technique could involve injuries as well as make you inefficient. To find out, you should look out for an experienced cook first once you start preparing your meals. Always make sure your knives are sharp as well. It could be much more hazardous if they are dull.

If you do not wish to take food preparation classes to learn about effective cutting techniques, you could also check out some food preparation programs on television and mirror exactly what they do.

It is vital to have a first-class chef's knife available. Preparing things like salads and soups, you will spend most of your time chopping. If you learn about the best ways to be an efficient cook, you could save a lot of time.

what is the Difference between Boiling, Heating, and Simmering?

These are three fundamental cooking techniques for the stovetop. Boiling is simply setting the heat on high and waiting for the blend to bubble. Compared to boiling, heating means letting it get hot without boiling. So, there are no bubbles produced with heating. Simmering means to have something stay on low heat for an extended time. As a rule, you use to simmer things like soups and stews.

what is the Difference between Baking and Broiling?

You should also differ between "baking" and "broiling" although there are meals that work well with both baking and broiling. With baking, things are put at a lower heat than with broiling. You might think about bread, cookies, cakes, and savory dishes such as vegetarian lasagne and roasted vegetables. Meals like vegetarian lasagne could also be broiled.

Generally, most ovens provide a broiler as well. However, before starting make sure to read the instructions carefully to take full advantage of the device.

take full advantage of Your kitchen inventory

One more critical step to producing vegan meals is to ensure you recognize ways to use all your devices. For instance, you may not know it but your microwave may additionally have a convection oven setup. You may not know about its full potential until you read through the handbook.

Moreover, you will have the ability to make changes in dishes based on the devices you have available. For instance, if the recipe requires something to be beaten on high for two minutes, your blender could take much longer if the "higher" setup is not as highly effective as the mixer that had been originally used to test and compose the initial dish.

Cooking Terms and their Meanings

Once you become familiar with your kitchen area and start preparing your first dishes, you may stumble upon some terms that you do not understand. Below are some common ones you may run into:

Mashing

You could either mash with your fork if it is a smaller-sized part or with a masher device. Some individuals like to whip things that are normally mashed such as potatoes or squash.

Whip

You could make use of a hand mixer, upright mixer, or a wire whisk to whip nearly anything.

Pulverize

You can crush things with the rear of your knife, the bottom of a glass, or various other heavy things. There are likewise unique kitchen devices that are used for pulverizing.

Grate

Graters are available in different forms. Just make your choice. If you should grate an orange cover or lemon peel, a small handheld grater is most ideal.

Knife Techniques

There are many various types of knife techniques you can follow such as chopping, julienne technique (matchstick-sized pieces, crush, and slice).

Mix

Depending on your mixture you have three options - an ordinary blender, a hand-held submersion mixer that works ideal for soups, and a food processor. The device you use relies on the dish you want to prepare.

Puree

When a recipe requires something to be pureed, you can do it in little batches in the regular blender, use a submersion mixer, or make use of a food processor.

This is just an overview of some of the strategies you will certainly come across. A cookbook will assist you to find out other terms you need to know. Alternatively, you could look online.

5

preparing a vegan MEAL might be a challenge

Being a vegan does not imply you will be automatically slim and incredibly healthy and balanced. This is true because it is still possible to take too many calories as a vegan, despite the wealth of nutrient foods to select from. So, every initiative should be taken to create well-balanced meals.

Of course, this can be an obstacle, particularly if you are just at the beginning of this lifestyle. One explanation for this is that specific minerals and vitamins, such as vitamin B12 and iron, are a lot more found in meat products. In addition, iron is more readily absorbed in the body when paired with meat.

RULES FOR A PERFECT VEGAN DIET

This chapter will cover a few of the difficulties vegans usually experience when putting dishes together. It is written to assist you in preparing healthy and balanced dish combinations that will keep you energetic. If you wish to slim down or remain thin, just do not forget to avoid too many calories with your meals.

Protein Is Crucial

Usually, people who use to eat meat regularly can easily cover their necessary protein intake. All they have to do is consume dairy products and a slice or two of meat or fish a day to replenish their iron store. However, as vegans do not eat meat, they will need to get their share of iron from different sources. The good news is that there are sources around the plant world that are still rich in protein:

Soy products

Nuts, seeds, nut milk, and nut butter

Grains, especially quinoa

Legumes such as kidney beans

You might also intend to drink a serving or two of protein beverages each day. However, before you do so, make sure the product packaging suggests it is vegan-friendly. A typical ingredient you often use to find in many healthy protein powders is whey, which stems from milk. So, vegans should stay away from it.

Your Iron Store Should Be Fully Replenished

For women, getting sufficient amounts of iron is enough of a challenge. For a vegan, it is even more challenging. That is why lots of vegans tend to have iron deficiencies. If you should be among them, you should consider asking your doctor for advice. He might recommend taking an iron supplement. You can find plant-based, vegan-friendly iron supplements at the natural food shop. Moreover, make sure to eat these foods:

Spinach

Green beans

Brewer's yeast (a supplement)

Wheat germ

Lima beans

Dried fruit such as raisins and prunes

Cooking in a cast-iron skillet

Blackstrap molasses (use in baking or take as a supplement)

To make plant-based protein a lot more absorbable, mix it with a supplement C-rich meal or beverage. For instance, you could have a small glass of orange with a meal that contains a great deal of iron.

Never Miss Out On B-Vitamins

As a rule, vegans do not have to be afraid to miss out on B-vitamins because grains are an excellent source of those vitamins. However, getting enough vitamin B 12 could prove to be a challenge. The only way to make sure vegans do not run out of this crucial vitamin is to supplement it with a vegan-friendly variation of B-12, which is typically synthetic. Some cereals and beverages, however, contain B 12, too.

Foods Rich In Calcium Should Be On Your List

As for calcium, it is much easier compared to ever for a vegan to get their share of calcium. Below are some foods that should always be on your list:

Soy milk, nut milk, and rice milk are frequently paired with calcium. Make sure the product is vegan-friendly and includes a good quantity of calcium.

Nuts such as hazelnuts and almonds are also an excellent source of calcium.

Leafy green veggies and other vegetables such as bok choy, collard greens, turnip greens, and okra are likewise rich in calcium.

Anytime you prepare vegetables, it is highly recommended not to boil them unless you intend to drink the water as well. Most part of the calcium leaves the food during the cooking process by entering into the water.

HOW TO AVOID HEALTH ISSUES WHEN EATING VEGAN

On the one hand, choosing a new diet could be regarded as discomfort and a major headache. On the other hand, opting for a new lifestyle and transforming your whole eating behavior is a completely different story. It can be a quite enjoyable and interesting time in your life. However, it is also definitely a time in your life that will require a bit of initiative to make the best decisions. Many ways adopting a brand-new lifestyle could go wrong, particularly when you are altering dramatically the meals that you eat.

Generally, anyone who decides to live the vegan lifestyle will mostly succeed if he or she is serious about it. Of course, it takes some effort to remain healthy, so it will generally call for a bit of initiative. There is a wide range of nutrients that are provided in meats and various other animal products that you have to take to be healthy and balanced. If you just count on a vegan way of life without making sure to take other nutrients and vitamins that you are then missing out on, you will soon experience that your immune system starts deteriorating. Paying very close attention to exactly what you are consuming, and more significantly what you are missing out on is important.

The majority of individuals who are planning to adopt a brand-new way of living tend to do this for a long time or permanently. In this case, you simply cannot afford to skip any vital vitamins and nutrients. So, it is extremely important to learn about the appropriate meals you need to eat to remain as healthy as possible. The difference between a new way of living and a new diet regimen is a diet, which is not intended to be followed permanently. You are merely on a diet for a short time, in which you intend to meet your objectives. A lifestyle is something that you intend to stay with, which is why imperfections in a way of living have a much more hazardous impact compared to a disadvantage in a diet.

Speaking to your physician is also very vital. This will help you determine any kind of particular demands that you might have. This would be necessary because you never understand which nutrients are essential for you and your specific necessities until you learn about exactly what kind of physical condition you are presently in. For most people, there are few serious necessities when beginning, but learning about any kind of major troubles ahead of time is always a great idea to see your medical professional. This way, you can feel comfortable whatever may come.

The most challenging issue that you will probably have is the necessity to seek lots of nutrients. This is essential since it will assist you in maintaining your energy level and make sure you are not missing out on the nutrients to keep you as healthy and balanced as possible. If you miss this crucial step, it will be virtually difficult for you to sustain the way of life that you are attempting to adapt to.

So, you will have to plan that you always get your necessary share of nutrients. If you fail to plan, then you plan to fail. Correct planning will certainly allow you to enjoy your venture of a vegan lifestyle.

Talking with your medical professional about any type of worries that you have, along with doing a comprehensive medical examination to make sure that you are fully aware of any sort of potential issues before they happen, will certainly be a key when it comes to determining in advance if you can live the vegan life successfully or not. Every year there are lots of people who adopted a vegan way of life. You can also join these people in living a healthier and greener way of living. Small changes to your way of living could have a significant impact as long as you are careful and make smart choices. Breakout decisions, however, can be quite derogatory for your general wellness. That is why it is essential to plan if you choose the vegan way of life to be your new lifestyle.

what is next?

If you have been a vegan for a while, you might have adopted this lifestyle by now. Otherwise, you might want to plan a few of your meals ahead of time until you feel at ease with that, too. Even if you have been a vegan for some time, it is still recommendable to step back, so to speak, and decide to prepare some dishes in advance. This will not only guarantee that you get the proper share of nutrients you need, but it also helps to vary your dishes because you can plan meals around brand-new ingredients.

Besides preparing dishes, you can likewise keep a food diary. In it, keep track of what you eat, how you exactly prepared it, whether you liked it or not, and if you would change anything next time. It is also an excellent way to see if you get the right amount of nutrients. You do not need to make entire inquiries about that. Simply take a short inventory to make sure you are not missing out on some crucial ingredients.

It is recommended to take a multivitamin supplement along with consuming a healthy and balanced diet plan. This will ensure your body has what it needs to keep you energetic.

you are closer to VEGAN CUISINEs than you might think

There is a wide range of vegetarian cuisines resulting in a variety of delicious vegan dishes you can enjoy.

Here is a shortlist of some of the cuisines out there that might not have come to your mind yet:

Indian

The Indian cuisine offers a lot of grain and vegetable-based meals.

Chinese

The Buddhist monks use to live on vegetarian food.

French

This Mediterranean cuisine is distinguished by fresh fruits and tasty vegetables.

Italian

Fresh fruits and vegetables are also a crucial part of Italian cuisine.

Korean

Rice and vegetables belong to the favorite dishes in Korean cuisine and are consumed almost daily.

Thai

It uses plant-based food. Thai also packs some heat.

Vietnamese

Same as the Thai cuisine

Greek

Another Mediterranean region cuisine that uses fresh fruits and vegetables.

Of course, this list is not complete but should give you an idea that vegan cuisines might be closer to you than you might have thought. For instance, Mediterranean cuisine is generally a vegan-friendly cuisine because it focuses on plant-based foods. There are a lot of countries around the Mediterranean area, such as France, Italy, Greece, Spain, Morocco, and Algeria.

By the way, Asian cuisine is also famous for plant-based foods.

YOU ARE IN GOOD COMPANY: FAMOUS CELEBRITIES AND VEGAN COOKING

If you believe that a vegan lifestyle is something that just weird-looking people do who resemble the hippies from the 1960s, you are quite incorrect. There are a lot of very popular people who have adopted a vegan lifestyle. What is rather surprising is that several of them are not known for being vegan, but this is merely further evidence that just because you happen to eat vegan does not indicate you are going to be an outsider.

Many movie stars succeeded in living a vegan lifestyle. Among them are people such as Alicia Silverstone, Joaquin Phoenix, Lindsay Wagner, Natalie Portman, and Pamela Anderson. As you can see, some very famous actors are vegans. Pamela Anderson and also Alicia Silverstone have been large supporters of this lifestyle. As for Pamela Anderson, she has gone to some harsh lengths to speak about cruelty against animals and has also voiced displeasure with Kentucky Fried Chicken.

There are even many singers who are known for being vegans as well, such as Brandy, Bryan Adams, Chrissie Hynde, Rikki Rocket, Rick Rubin, Steve Jocz from Amount 41, and Weird Al Yankovic. A final artist who is very popular is the artist previously referred to as Prince. This is an impressive listing of some very famous people who take pleasure in a healthy and balanced vegan lifestyle.

Even among a lot of athletes, you will find vegans as well. There is Sally Eastall, an Olympic marathon runner, as well as Pat Reeves, who is a prizewinning powerlifter. In addition, there is also Judith Shakeshaft, a prizewinning mountain biker and runner. Carl Lewis, a sportsman who is self-confident enough to stand up proudly and proclaim to be vegan. While you might have never considered athletes to be the sort of people to live a vegan way of life, it is remarkable to find out that vegans can come from all corners of life.

Among those well-known stars, actresses, singers, and even sportsmen, there are a lot of very popular people who are providing veganism the audience, promotion, and respect it deserves. It is quite refreshing to see how these celebrities use their popularity to promote this healthy and balanced vegan lifestyle.

There are even lots of various political leaders who are vegans as well. As you can see by now, you are surrounded by very popular people who are happy to keep company with you when it comes to living the vegan lifestyle. The number of individuals who are engaging in veganism is continuously rising so you happen to join a famous group of individuals. Trying to make your unique mark on the globe may seem difficult. However, this group of actors, actresses, singers, athletes, and politicians prove that every person can cause a change. Even if they should only inspire an individual with the choice they made, it would be one more person to be counted among the vegans around the globe.

6

vegan cooking in special cases

The vegan diet plan is an optimal one for building and maintaining wellness and health. As stated in a previous chapter, it is still feasible to become overweight as a vegan because all you need to do is eat too many calories. It could even turn out to be a harmful lifestyle as a vegan if you miss out on crucial nutrients your body needs. Nevertheless, those issues can be quickly dealt with by cutting calories and preparing healthier dishes.

Nonetheless, some individuals face serious health issues they need to deal with. Some may be using the vegan diet regimen to help them recover their wellness. Others opted to be vegans for other reasons.

Listed here is a checklist of some usual health afflictions and ways to adjust the vegan diet regimen to fit in these cases. Remember that the vegan diet plan is a healthy and balanced diet regimen to start with so it makes these changes a whole lot easier.

LOW-SODIUM COOKING

Individuals who adhere to the vegan diet plan are equally prone to consume way too much salt as anyone else. In its purest state, the vegan diet is supposed to be low in sodium. However, if you should grab the salt shaker too often, it will have a derogatory impact on your health and wellness.

Packaged and processed meals are everywhere available regardless if you should happen to be a vegan or not. This is also definitely true for the salt shaker. Prevent it, particularly if you have a propensity to preserve water or if you suffer from hypertension.

LOW-FAT DIET

If you follow the vegan diet plan, you are going to profit from a diet that is low in fat. To be more exact, since you are not supposed to consume any type of meat, the vegan diet is low in saturated fats and high in the more valuable unsaturated fats that come from avocado, nuts and seeds, and various veggie oils.

Nonetheless, there is also a third type of fat you should always avoid, which are trans fats. In most cases, these are even worse for you compared to saturated fats. Likewise, you may also need to include a small number of saturated fats in your diet plan. The best and healthiest way to get your proper intake of saturated fats is by consuming coconut from time to time. You can also prepare with coconut oil, which could take the place of butter or lard.

LOW-SUGAR COOKING

If you adhere to the vegan diet plan as it is suggested to be complied with, the vegan diet regimen is normally a low-sugar diet. Nevertheless, as with any lifestyle, there is the opportunity that you could overdo it. Of course, your body cannot work properly without sugar. However, there is a healthy and a less healthy way to get your proper share of it. You can get it normally from fresh and dried fruits and also from maple syrup, sugar canes, or rice syrup.

Nonetheless, there are also baked items and various other sweet opportunities (such as vegan-friendly chocolate) that might turn out to be equally addictive as their non-vegan equivalents. What applies to most areas in life is also true in this special case: Moderation is the secret. If you wish to comply with a low-sugar diet plan, help your body to enjoy sugar in its natural state where it exists in fruit, and not to take pleasure in baked foods.

DIABETES

There are two types of diabetic issues - Type 1, which people are born with, and Type 2, which uses to come later in life. The vegan diet regimen should be a low-fat one and is specifically useful for people who suffer from Type 2 diabetic issues. However, Type 1 patients can also profit from it.

If you stay with slim foods, whole grains, legumes, nuts, seeds, and a lot of fruits and vegetables, you will be able to fix your health issues quite naturally. Additionally, make sure to take the medicine you are expected to. When your body is not able to produce the hormone insulin or not enough of it, you will have to get it from outside your body meaning by injections.

DISEASES OF THE CIRCULATORY SYSTEM

Illnesses concerning the blood circulation system, such as higher cholesterol, hypertension, and heart issues, all benefit from the vegan diet regimen in a very natural way. This is true because the vegan diet is a low-fat and low-cholesterol diet. Likewise, if you have hypertension, you could take an extra step and avoid consuming too much salt.

So, this is one more situation where adhering to the vegan diet, as you typically would, improves your health and could help you naturally deal with these issues.

GLUTEN-FREE COOKING

When you first start as a vegan, it might seem quite a challenge to avoid all the gluten "traps" you are constantly subject to fall into. You can still be very successful with mastering this challenge as well. So, in case you are looking for ways to avoid gluten, you should make sure that the following grains are no part of your diet:

Oats

Barley

Wheat

Rye

Kamut

Spelt

Do not get discouraged after going through this list as there are other grains and starches you can enjoy eating instead such as:

Rice, especially brown rice

Quinoa

Corn

Millet

Potatoes

Please make sure to stick to these grains and starches to exclude gluten from your diet.

As you could learn in this chapter, it is very feasible to live a vegan lifestyle even if should deal with a wide range of health issues. Moreover, this lifestyle could even help alleviate many of your health problems in a way you would have never thought possible.

7

VEGAN COOKING FOR SPECIAL PEOPLE

is vegan cooking good for children?

Given the rising popularity of a vegan lifestyle all over the world, it is not surprising many moms and dads are beginning to consider whether their children should follow a vegan diet plan as well. If you should be right now in this position and pondering if a vegan diet is suitable for your children, rest assured: You are not alone.

Yearly, there is a significant increase of hundreds of people who make up their mind to switch to a vegan diet, and in many cases, they use to bring their children in, too. If you should have serious doubts about the impact of a vegan diet on your children, do not hesitate to consult your physician. However, in general, most children do quite well with a vegan diet plan as long as a couple of preventative measures are considered.

Your first step ought to be examining your dietary understanding. If you have poor knowledge of nutrition, then it will be far more difficult for you to figure out if you are qualified to meet your youngsters' dietary requirements. While the majority of moms and dads fret about not providing their youngsters proper nourishment, this concern becomes more vital if you feed your youngsters a vegan diet since many nutrients can be very easily neglected if you are not watching over the nutritional quest of your children very carefully.

If you should still have any questions about what your child requires for nutritional balance, it is time to join either a dietary lesson or to start looking online for some clear information on exactly what you should concentrate on. A proper understanding of nourishment will certainly make it possible for your kids to eat a vegan diet while still getting each of the nutrients that are required. It is very crucial to watch over the nutritional intake carefully. Many novice vegans tend to overlook this issue and thus miss out on necessary nutrients that are essential to proper and healthy nourishment. If you have made up your mind to live a vegan way of life, then make also sure to take a vitamin supplement regularly.

If you want your children to have a great start with living as a vegan, you should make sure to keep encouraging your children to eat lots of delicious foods. Very often, children tend to eat few fruits and vegetables in normal life. However, if you are encouraging a healthy way of life as a vegan, you have to make sure that your children are quite aware that consuming sufficient vegetables and fruits to provide them adequate nutrients is crucial. This is not always easy to do, especially if your children are in the habit of consuming meats. However, if you accustom your kids to a vegan lifestyle once your child is first starting to eat solid food, you will discover that it is considerably easier to form this habit.

A lot of moms and dads find that their kids' biggest challenge is to give up on meat. This is simply a fact since a lot of kids are not subject to change their habits, especially their eating habits. This is also true when it comes to changing the small food habits of your children. Even changing these small eating habits, could make a child rebel in a way you might not have anticipated. So, to guarantee that you are getting the very best results possible, you ought to cooperate with your children instead of trying to compel them to eat a diet regimen that they are not excited about. Small things such as a good attitude could have a great influence when it comes to providing your youngsters the nutrients that they truly need.

As a rule, a vegan diet could allow your kids to consume precisely what you are eating without any kind of significant issues and difficulties. However, it is vital to understand that you might also need to provide your youngsters with ample nutritional supplements to shield them from dietary deficiencies. Few issues of nutritional deficiencies could result in substantial difficulties if you are trying to live a vegan way of life without seriously watching over the nutritional requirements that you need to have met. A well-planned way of living could properly allow you to integrate a vegan way of living for even children while still staying healthy. If you take the time and effort to switch over to the vegan lifestyle, you could easily master all challenges you may face after starting.

WHAT ABOUT VEGAN COOKING WHILE PREGNANT?

Having a child is an amazing time in the lives of most people, and trying to remain healthy is to be considered a top priority for the majority of people. Attempting to carry out pregnancy successfully while complying with a vegan way of living, might look overwhelming at first glance. However, if a pregnant woman does not face any critical health issues, it is quite feasible to adopt a vegan lifestyle even during pregnancy. Nevertheless, there are a couple of considerations that you need to be aware of to obtain the most effective results possible.

As a rule, the average woman undergoing typical maternity is not subject to face any major issues with her pregnancy. This might seem for many women like a dream they wish to come true. Admittedly, the majority of women do face at least some mild troubles throughout their pregnancy, which makes it a bit tough to have the hassle-free maternity they wish for. You are not the only one if you have experienced some problems. However, if you are vegan, it is extremely important to make sure that you are provided, along with your child, with the proper nutrients you and your child need.

It is essential to tell your doctor that you are vegan once you start the prenatal treatment, so your doctor can discuss your specific dietary needs as well as carefully watch you and your child obtaining the outcomes required. Some women face no difficulties when it comes to gaining the proper weight. However, others require assistance gaining the right weight while others require help to make sure they do not gain too much of it. There are lots of means that your physician can help you with, but without understanding your regular consuming behaviors he will probably fail to do so.

For this purpose, you should take some time to write down every one of the meals that you consume. This will enable your medical professional to swiftly and easily see if there is anything that you should be consuming that you are not currently eating. Additionally, taking a multi-vitamin is critical. This will assist you to make sure that any sort of deficiency you may have is resolved. Taking actions to remain healthy is much better compared to waiting until you face a health issue you will need to take care of. This is particularly true if you are pregnant because your objective is to make sure that your infant also remains healthy.

You might believe it or not, it is possible to carry an infant to full term while consuming a vegan diet regimen. You may have to take a bit of additional effort to prepare meals, but annually there are hundreds of vegan maternities. You could also join the ladies who start and complete their pregnancies as a vegan.

Attempting to raise your children as a vegan right from maternity is an excellent start for their lives and could also provide them some great advantages, too.

Putting in the time to discuss your diet demands with your doctor is important to make sure that you continue to be healthy and balanced. Moreover, make sure to consume enough calories to cover your needs as well as the needs of your infant. This will certainly help to nourish your child sufficiently. Of course, not getting enough calories is not a problem that is special to veganism but rather quite independent of nutritional habits.

Having healthy and balanced infants is not dependent upon the diet plan you prefer to comply with. Speaking to your doctor and making sure that you are eating appropriately are all the basic actions that you have to take, which will certainly be very effective in helping you achieve your goal of a happy and, most importantly, healthy baby. Skimping over critical nutrients is not advised no matter which nutritional route you are intending to take.

8

Putting it all together: recommendations on RECIPES

Okay, if you have read so far, you might be curious about how to put all together what you have learned by now. This chapter is intended to give you some ideas on recipes to start your vegan journey as soon as possible. It is up to you to alter or adapt these recommendations on recipes if you see they fit better.

If you just started your vegan diet, it is advised to keep a cooking journal. It should include the recipes you have been excited about and those that had not been after your fancy. The cooking journal makes things easier when it comes to remembering what you liked to replicate it any time you want. And it also gives you the chance to make adjustments to those recipes that you did not like when you first prepared them. So, let us start with some of these delicious recipes:

APPETIZERS

1) Bruschetta

This is a classic Italian appetizer or snack, which is completely vegan and a great starting point for your vegan menu.

Ingredients:

¼ cup scallions, chopped

1 large tomato, diced

1 clove garlic, minced

1 tablespoon dried basil

6 slices fresh, whole-grain bakery bread

Olive oil

Instructions:

Preheat oven to 350 degrees. In a small mixing bowl, combine the first four ingredients. Spray a baking sheet with non-stick cooking spray and arrange bread sliced on the sheet. Spoon tomato mixture evenly over all four slices. Drizzle with olive oil. Bake for about 15 minutes, or until bread is toasted.

2) Black Olive Hummus

Hummus is also a classic vegetarian food, which is low in fat and high in protein. Spread on whole grain, vegan crackers, or serve with bread.

Ingredients:

1,15 oz can cooked chickpeas, drained and rinsed

1 tablespoon water, 1/3 cup fresh lemon juice

1/4 cup pitted black olives, diced

Instructions:

Combine all the ingredients in a mixer or blender and pulse until they become creamy. Transfer to a serving meal and serve with crackers, bread, or whole-grain pita wedges.

SOUPS

1) Greek Style Chickpea Soup

This is an example of a hearty Greek meal, which is vegan-friendly. Serve with slices of fresh, whole-grain bread and a salad.

Ingredients:

3,15-ounce cans of chickpeas, drained and rinsed

1 large onion, chopped

1 teaspoon dried rosemary

3 tablespoons fresh, chopped parsley

1 teaspoon sea salt

4 cloves garlic, chopped fine

1,28-ounce can-crushed tomatoes (keep the juice)

3 cups water

2 tablespoons olive oil

Salt and pepper to taste

Instructions:

Add all the ingredients to a large pot. Boil them, then simmer on low for an hour until flavors are well mixed. You can also cook it in a crockpot on the low setting for 4-6 hours.

2) Classic Minestrone Soup

This soup is very popular and could be a great starting point for your meal. The cool thing about it is that you can use whichever vegetables you just happen to have available.

Ingredients:

2 large carrots, peeled and chopped

3 celery stalks, chopped

1 medium onion, chopped

2 cloves garlic, minced

2 zucchini, chopped

1 cup broccoli florets

1 cup spinach leaves

1 can crushed tomatoes

1 cup canned kidney beans, rinsed

8 cups water

1 cup small pasta like elbows or orzo

Salt and pepper to taste

Fresh chopped parsley for a garnish

Instructions:

Combine all the ingredients except for the pasta in a soup pot. Boil them and then simmer for at least one hour until the vegetables are soft. Add pasta during the last fifteen minutes of cooking and cook for eight to ten minutes. You can also cook the soup in the crockpot. Just add all the ingredients at once.

SALADS

1) Vegan Cesar Salad

The Cesar salad is a classic. Unfortunately, however, the dressing is not vegan-friendly. So, let us make some adjustments to the recipe.

Ingredients For The Dressing:

1/2 cup vegan mayonnaise

1/2 cup brewer's yeast

Juice of 1 lemon

2 teaspoons cracked pepper

Ingredients For The Salad:

4 cups torn romaine lettuce leaves

1 cup chopped black olives

3 tablespoons grated soy cheese

Instructions:

At the bottom of a large salad bowl, whisk all the salad dressing ingredients together. Toss in the romaine lettuce until dressing is well coated. Top with black olives and soy cheese and serve.

2) Classic Salad

The classic salad is by nature vegan-friendly. Just choose the vegetables and the vegetables which you want as long as they are vegan. You can make your vegan dressings, too. Vinaigrettes are especially easy since all they require is equal parts of oil and vinegar whisked together. You can also add salt, pepper, and spices to taste.

Salads are nice because you can use whatever you have in the house. Keep your refrigerator well-stocked so you can make a healthy salad whenever you want.

MAIN COURSES

1) Vegan Lentil Tacos

Lentils are a good alternative for traditional beef, which is usually found in tacos.

Ingredients:

1 cup dried, brown lentils

1,8 ounce can of tomato sauce

1 packet taco seasoning mix (vegan)

Corn tortillas or taco shells

Shredded romaine lettuce

Cucumber slices

Chopped, fresh tomatoes

Soy sour cream

Salsa

Guacamole

Instructions:

Soak the lentils in a large bowl until they become soft for about one hour. Transfer to a saucepan and blend with tomato sauce and taco seasoning. Add about ¼ cup of water. Simmer on low until it is heated through. Spoon into taco shells or tortillas and top with things like sour cream, salsa, lettuce, cucumber, and tomato.

2) Healthy Vegetable Casserole

Casseroles are another healthy dinner alternative for vegans. The nice thing about them is once you have the recipe down pat, you can make further adjustments whenever you see it fit.

Ingredients:

1 cup cooked brown rice

1,8 ounce can of tomato soup

1,8 ounce can legumes such as chickpeas or kidney beans

4 cups vegetables of choice – try zucchini, mushrooms, carrots, celery, eggplant, tomatoes, leeks, onions, garlic, potatoes

Instructions:

Spray a medium casserole meal with non-stick cooking spray. Layer with brown rice. Add vegetables on top of the rice. You can blend the vegetables, choose one type of vegetable, or layer different kinds – whatever you prefer. Pour soup over vegetables. Cover and bake at 350 degrees for 45 minutes and you are done.

<u>**SIDE DISHES**</u>

When it comes to side dishes, there are a lot of options you can consider. Here are some ideas you could start with:

1) Cover a baking sheet with vegetables such as carrots, zucchini, eggplant, asparagus, and parsnips. Sprinkle with olive oil, salt, and paper and bake at 400 degrees until it is soft.

2) You can add water or vegetable stock to cooked squash, cauliflower, or potatoes and mash or whip. Use salt and pepper to taste. By the way, miso broth works especially well.

3) Serve a nice salad as a side dish or sticks of fresh vegetables.

4) Choose your favorite grain, such as quinoa, millet, or couscous, and follow the package directions. Season with salt and pepper and serve with your main course. You can also add vegetables and herbs to give it more nutritional value.

5) Do not forget pickled vegetables – these make a nice alternative to standard side dishes.

Use your imagination. You can also serve fruit as a side dish, or vegan apple sauce.

<u>**DESSERTS**</u>

Vegan Brownies

Before starting you should make sure that all of these ingredients are vegan-friendly. It might surprise you, but you do not have to miss out on chocolate since there is also vegan chocolate available!

Ingredients:

1 cup white flour

1 cup whole-wheat flour

1 cup water

1 cup brown sugar

1 teaspoon salt

1 teaspoon vanilla extract

¾ cup cocoa powder for baking

½ cup vegetable oil

½ teaspoon baking powder

<u>Optional</u>: ½ -1 cup chopped nuts, ½ -1 cup chocolate chips

Instructions:

Spray a 9 x 13 baking sheet with non-stick cooking spray. Combine flour, water, brown sugar, and salt. (a wire whisk works best for this purpose). Stir in vanilla extract, cocoa, vegetable oil, and baking powder using a wooden spoon. Spread evenly into the baking sheet and bake at 400 for about 30 minutes, until a toothpick inserted on the sides comes out clean.

Things To Do With Fresh Fruit

Fresh fruits are always a good idea to combine with a nice dessert. You can serve it by itself, or you can make it part of the following options:

1) Make a fresh fruit salad with your favorite seasonal fruits. Season the salad with citrus juice.

2) Top fresh fruit with vanilla soy yogurt

3) Add fresh fruit such as chopped apples to a small baking dish. Top with walnuts, brown sugar, and cinnamon and bake at 350 until apples are soft.

4) Do the same as above, but try pears, peaches, blueberries, or varieties of apples instead. You can also experiment with the nuts and the spices. This makes a nice substitute for apple, pear, blueberry, or peach cobbler, or crisp.

5) Grill fresh pineapple slices or bananas. Slice the banana in half crosswise and sprinkle with cinnamon.

As you see, there are lots of ways to prepare vegan dishes. This list is intended to give you a slight idea of the various possibilities you will learn about yourself once you get started to live as a vegan.

9

CONCLUSION

So, by now you should have a very good idea of what you can expect from a vegan life. You should have a thorough understanding of what it means to be vegan. Let us shortly sum up the things that have been covered within this book:

1) How to stock your pantry

2) Hidden ingredients to avoid

3) An understanding of basic cooking techniques

4) Typical foods that make up a vegan diet

5) How to put together healthy meals

6) Adapting the vegan diet for different health issues

7) Some new recipes

Whatever your reasons are to start living out the vegan lifestyle, this book has been created as a source that is meant to help you achieve a completely vegan and healthy way of life as soon and as effortlessly as possible.

The vegan lifestyle truly represents a dedication to boosting your health if you are willing to make the necessary adjustments in your diet plan. This diet route could virtually take you to levels of health and wellness you have never thought possible. It could turn out to become your highway to health.

Besides, living a vegan lifestyle is also a social choice for a lot of people who are committed to it. If you wish to decrease your influence on the environment, make sure to buy organic food and avoid genetically modified foods.

So, the vegan way of life could have a huge impact on both your health and the environment for many years to come. If you decide to live as a vegan, you will discover that it is much easier to live healthier by following the vegan diet plan. You should not miss your chance to find that out. Make the maintenance of your health your top priority and find out whether living as a vegan could be the route you should be taken to achieve that goal as long as you live.

ABOUT THE AUTHOR

Dr. Robertino Bedenian resides in Frankfurt, Germany. He is a fitness instructor accredited by the German Olympic Committee teaching aerobics, back gymnastics, stretching, and power gymnastics. He has a website about the vegan lifestyle covering diet and health recommendations (goingveganhealthbenefits.com), detoxication programs, fitness guidelines, and disease-related topics. In his book "Going Vegan – How to Vegan Without Going Crazy", he gives answers to those people who are seriously considering to get involved in the vegan lifestyle but have been kept from adopting this revolutionary diet habit due to so many questions that they still need to be answered. This book is intended to give a comprehensive overview of what it is like to live as a vegan. It is created to show you the best way how to start your vegan journey, how to avoid the traps every novice of a vegan lifestyle could very easily fall into, and how to achieve your goal healthy and effortlessly. After reading this book you should have a very distinguished knowledge of a vegan lifestyle. Of course, it will also give you some great recommendations on recipes for a vegan diet that you do not want to miss. It is written in a very simple and understandable way, so there is no background knowledge necessary to reap the full benefits of this book.

Don't miss out!

Visit the website below and you can sign up to receive emails whenever Dr. Robertino Bedenian publishes a new book. There's no charge and no obligation.

https://books2read.com/r/B-A-YQGQ-TTBSB

BOOKS2READ

Connecting independent readers to independent writers.

Also by Dr. Robertino Bedenian

Fitness Over 60 For Women – How to Stay Fit And Healthy As You Age
Does Back Pain Go Away? 10 Answers To The Most Acute Back Pain Issues
Massage Bible - A Beginners Guide To Western And Eastern Massage Therapy
Going Vegan - How To Vegan Without Going Crazy
Chiropraktik - Was Steckt Eigentlich Dahinter?
Massagen: Ein Überblick Über Westliche Und Östliche Massagetechniken
Natuerlich Abnehmen, Schlank Und Endlich Fit Sein
P.S. Ich Liebe Dich: Wenn Liebe So Einfach Wäre
Was Tun Bei Rückenschmerzen, Bandscheibenvorfall Und Ischiasschmerzen:
10 Antworten Zu Den Häufigsten Fragen Bei Rückenschmerzen
Was Tun Gegen Schlafapnoe, Schlafstörungen Und Schnarchen
Self-Help Books for Women
Diabetes How to Help: Everything You Need to Know About Diabetes Type
1 and Type 2
Diet and Workout Planner: How to Stay Healthy and Get Fit for Life
Everything I Know About Love
The Sleep Easy Solution Book: How to Stop Sleep Apnea, Snoring, and Sleep
Disorders
Your Super Gut Feeling Restored – How to Restore Your Life Energy and
Overall Health from The Inside Out

Watch for more at https://booksummarypublishing.com.

About the Author

Dr. Robertino Bedenian is a qualified fitness instructor accredited by the German Olympic Committee, a health and nutrition expert, and the author of several books on diet, health, and fitness!

For more than twenty years he has been a fitness coach at the sports university teaching aerobics, back gymnastics, stretching, high-intensity interval training (HIIT), power gymnastics, and athletic sports.

On his website, he has published more than 300 articles about the vegan lifestyle covering diet and health recommendations, detoxication programs, fitness guidelines, and disease-related topics. He is part of a family with an orthopedic surgeon, a physical therapist, an osteopath, and an alternative practitioner.

He is also the founder of the brand "**Going Vegan**" selling high-quality supplements for optimal health.

You are more than welcome to check his website for more details: https://goingveganhealthbenefits.com.

His brand has been awarded continuously with 5-star feedback by customers for its outstanding product quality.

Dr. Bedenian is also the founder of the book company "**Book Summary Publishing**" publishing summaries and workbooks of Amazon #1 bestselling non-fiction books.

If you want to learn more about the summaries and workbooks that he has published so far, please visit his website:

https://booksummarypublishing.com
Read more at https://booksummarypublishing.com.